Thunder Shamanism
The Indo-European
Medicine Wheel

An Initiation Into Thunder Shamanism

by

Michael William Denney

ThunderShamanism.com

Introduction

Modern Homo Sapiens (Humans) are believed by Science to have emerged around 100,000 years ago in South Eastern Africa. According to the latest scientific opinions, modern Homo Sapiens were the first human species, perhaps the first creatures on planet Earth, who developed religious thought and ritual.

A climate change around 50,000 years ago that transformed the Sahara desert into a grassland savanna attracted grazing animals which attracted the first modern humans who then, being able to safely cross the Sahara plains, in successive waves, migrated out of Africa into the Northern Hemisphere for the first time in their history as a species.

These first modern humans entering the Middle East, Asia and Europe for the first time, brought with them their unique understanding of the Cosmos which spawned all of the ancestral religions and their descendants which are in existence today. These first ancestors of all people alive today followed a spiritual belief system which modern academia calls, "Animism." Animism comes from the Latin word "animus" which is often loosely translated as "spirit" or "consciousness."

Animism
Animism believes that all things in manifested reality whether they be plant, animal, rocks, insects, trees, clouds, mountains, oceans, thunder, rain, lightning, ghosts, spirits, illnesses and even ideas all possess an "animus" or a conscious spirit with which we humans can interact and communicate.

The Animist spiritual practitioner is someone who has been called by the ancestors to act as a conduit through which humans can communicate and interact with all the forces of Nature. An Animist practitioner in modern society is more commonly known as a "Shaman." The traditional shaman acted as an intermediary who helped the tribe locate food, game, water, shelter, as well as heal diseases of all kinds whether that be of a spiritual, mental or physical nature.

The Origin of The Terms "Shaman" and "Shamanism"

The word "shaman" is from the indigenous Siberian animist religion called "Tengerism." A shaman is a Tengerist priest or priestess who acts as an intermediary between the spiritual and physical realm. In order to be called a "shaman" in Tengerist society, one must be called by the ancestors and subsequently trained and initiated by a recognized Tengerist priest (master shaman) before one can rightly be called a shaman. This is also true for virtually every traditional animist practitioner worldwide throughout history whether they be called, Shaman, Wizard, Sifu, Witch, Guru, Magus, Babalawo, etc.,...

Technically speaking, it is inaccurate to use the term "shaman" outside of the Tengerist religion. Nevertheless, this is the word most commonly used in modern society when referring to any animist practitioners. The appropriation of this term goes back in the 18th century when European Christian missionaries traveled to Siberia and witnessed Tengerist priests (shamans) practicing their art. As a result, the European missionaries appropriated the terms "shaman" and "shamanism" to represent any and all forms of animist practices regardless of cultural or spiritual affiliation.

It is important that the reader understand that I do not wish to give the impression that I am teaching anything related to what is often referred to as "Native American Shamanism." I have not been formally trained by any Native Americans or Siberians for that matter. It is well known that many Native Americans take great offense at the use of the word "shamanism" in regard to their native practices. While it is true that Native American religions often contain animist concepts, that does not mean they are influenced by Siberian Tengerism. Therefore, Native practitioners are right in pointing out that their religions are not forms of shamanism.

Even though it is technically inaccurate to use the terms "shaman" and "shamanism" outside of the Tengerist culture, rightly or wrongly, these are the words most commonly understood in modern Western society to describe animism and animist practices. So for the sake of effective communication, I will use the terms "shaman" and "shamanism" in this modern anthropological fashion to describe the animist concepts and practices contained in this book.

My apologies for any unintended offense by my use of these terms. Even though I use these terms in this way, my main goal is to actually help repair the harm that has been done to Native practices in modern times by ignorant (albeit, well meaning) Westerners. One way to reverse this destructive trend is to educate modern Westerners of their own animist heritage. By doing so, this may reduce the numbers of people unintentionally causing offense to Natives by unknowingly adopting pseudo Native American practices in the honest attempt to connect to legitimate animist spirituality.

So, while I am knowingly misusing these terms in this book and in other books, videos and websites, I do so for the sole purpose of educating people in the animist concepts that were once shared by all peoples. I have considered replacing "Shaman" with "Animist" and "Shamanism" with "Animism", but since my goal is to educate as many Westerners as possible in their own animist heritage, it is expedient for me to use the terms with which they are most familiar in order to reach the greatest amount of people. Once,again, my apologies for any unintended offense by my use of these terms.

Animist Healing
The animist method of healing seeks to understand the nature of the imbalance causing the illness. The Shaman by means of communicating with the body, the ancestors, the spirits or even the disease itself uncovers methods and remedies whereby the patient can regain his/her natural state of balance which will result in harmony and health.

Animism sees manifested reality as a constantly shifting interplay of a myriad of forces involved in a dynamic dance of creation. Since all existence in animist belief is thought to contain a conscious spirit, the animist practitioner seeks to maintain a dynamic balance with these forces, which sometimes can seemingly act chaotically and destructively to humans. By communicating with these dynamically opposing forces, the shaman discovers the most beneficial ways in which he and his fellow humans can cooperate with the dance of Nature and achieve a temporary state of harmonious interdependence. Since all of the Cosmos is in constant motion and metamorphosis, the shaman understands that maintaining harmonious balance with the Cosmos is on-going endeavor which is renewed on a daily or even momentary basis.

This is a very long-winded way of me saying that Shamanism (Animism) is the original human religion. It is also a highly effective spiritual strategy for human survival that worked extremely well for at least 100,000 years.

But, very recently in human history, around two thousand years ago, human civilization made its official entry into the "modern" era which made a revolutionary and radical departure in religious thought. Humans began seeing themselves as being separate from their environment. They began to see the Natural World as being hostile to their very existence. This departure from our animist roots of seeing Humans as an integral part of all creation, created a massive shift in thinking and action which has had undeniable and in some cases, tragic, irreversible effects on all levels of existence.

After over 25 years of intense study, practice, instruction and research into various shamanic disciplines from around the globe (that retain an <u>unbroken connection into pre-history</u>), I believe I have discovered an underlying, universally applicable science of Life Force Energy that transcends culture, religion and ethnicity. It is my desire to share this knowledge with all those who wish to experience the power of Spirit with which the ancestors once knew and lived.

The Indo-Europeans
Since I have sub-titled this book "The Indo-European Medicine Wheel," I feel the need to address how I am using this term in this book. The term "Indo-European" (IE) describes primarily a linguistic connection among the majority of languages in Europe and in parts of the Middle East and Eurasia. I am not using this term in any ethnic sense. Recent developments in linguistics and DNA research have concluded that the languages that fall within the classification of "Indo-European" have their origins in Paleolithic Africa with a portion of the first modern humans who crossed the Sahara and migrated into the Northern Hemisphere.

That means that the first people who spoke this language were dark-skinned Africans who, over long stretches of time, adapted to changing environments in various places across the Northern Hemisphere. This occurred over a span of at least 50,000 years. That means that while the term "Indo-European" is most often associated with people of light skin and light eyes, and while that is indeed partially accurate, the first Indo-Europeans were dark-skinned Africans who, in various degrees and in various climates, over tens of thousands of years in Ice Age conditions, were slowly transformed in their appearance by their immediate climate. In those individuals who settled in the more northern areas of Europe, they transformed into what we now refer to as "white people." But regardless of the various modern appearances of all of the various Indo European ethnic groups in existence today, they all are descended from hearty travelers from Africa who, fifty thousand years ago, spoke the roots of Indo-European language and may have worshipped the same Indo-European gods as are found in much of ancient Indo-European mythology.

The speakers of the IE languages, who by this time had spread into a vast territory stretching from Northern Europe and eventually into Southern Asia (India), had independently adapted to such a varying degree of climates, that while their fundamental language, religion and culture had remained remarkably uniform and intact, the ethnic and genetic factors had changed considerably to the point that, from an ethnic perspective, after tens of thousands of years, these various IE peoples may not have even remotely resembled each other on a superficial physical viewing.

I state this to silence any fears that this book is in any way intended as a means of ethnic exclusion. My use of the term Indo-European is intended to connect me all the way back through my ancestral line stretching even to the origins of my people who were in fact, ethnic Africans. As a shaman, my job is to connect all the way back to the first people who carried with them the primal knowledge of the spirit realm, the men and women who were first to carry the teachings and wisdom of the Shining Ones or the gods.

In light of the immense span of time connected to the IE people, why am I focusing on this, perhaps somewhat arbitrary classification of Indo-European? I must admit that I have a personal attachment to finding the roots of shamanic practices of my own (IE) ancestors. As it happens, there is a surprising uniformity of understanding when different IE spiritual traditions are compared to one another. But, it would be misleading of me if I didn't inform the reader that I am also drawing significantly from other spiritual sources outside of the IE model. I considered sub-titling this book "The Universal Medicine Wheel" but I did not want to give the impression of providing the world with a book consisting of yet another new agey rehashing of pseudo-Native American styled fluff that has filled our bookstores for decades. I also use this term because I do feel that it is vitally important that the Western world, which has its roots in IE history and culture, re-embrace its ancestral IE spiritual and historical identity.

The obliteration of traditional, animist IE spiritual concepts from the Western world during the Middle Ages has resulted in a self-perpetuating spiritual emptiness within modern Western society. The result of this loss of our historic spiritual identity has forced those of us who wish to embrace indigenous shamanic paths to seek spiritual disciplines from outside of our own Western cultural framework.

This departure from modern Western spirituality has been absolutely necessary for modern shamanic seekers because it is a fact that Westerners completely abandoned their traditional animist world-view millennia ago and so we have no choice but to look to other cultures for legitimate shamanic practices. Unfortunately however, adopting the cultural context of those "exotic" spiritual pathways also has reinforced millennia-old psychological patterns among many of European descent creating feelings of spiritual inferiority, shame and self-hatred that, ironically, perpetuate racial and cultural stereotypes that continue to isolate us from the very indigenous spirituality that we so desperately crave.

In short, we need to remember that we Westerners are also descended from indigenous, primal, shamanic practitioners and this so-called "primitive" shamanic world-view rightly belongs to us too. With this understanding, it is not necessary to superficially adopt or appropriate the spiritual world view of other cultures unless we choose to do so. Unconsciously doing so in an attempt to escape the destructive limitations of our culture demeans everyone and creates a sense of hypocrisy and superficiality that can act as a hindrance to our spiritual progress.

I'm not advocating against adopting foreign spiritual disciplines, gods know I have studied them voraciously. I'm advocating that whatever paths we adopt should be done with deliberate, conscious awareness. They should be pursued, not as a means of escaping our Western heritage, but as a way to reawaken it.

(As I am writing this, new genetic evidence has arisen that indicates that the ethnic population that is most closely related to the first modern humans in Europe are the Scandinavians. I find this ironic because it is this "Nordic" stereotype of the blond haired, blue eyed "Aryan" that was used as a symbol of the Nazi racist propaganda machine to differentiate "white" people from other "darker" races. Yet, it is this "Nordic" ethnic population that retains the closest genetic link to those first African explorers who ventured into Ice Age Europe. Any modern racists who use their Nordic heritage as a

way to differentiate themselves from other ethnicities are in fact unwittingly acknowledging that their so called "Aryan" ethnicity is what links them most directly to their ancient African ancestors. And again, all this does for me is to underscore the deep self-hatred that has infected the modern Western psyche for the past two millenia.)

The world has been happy to explore traditional Indo-European spiritual concepts in television, video games and in such films as "The Lord of The Rings" which, unbeknownst to most, are entirely based on pre-Christian, polytheist, Norse mythology. The world is ready to incorporate these traditional IE spiritual beliefs and values into the patch-work of the spiritual melting pot of world religions. Our traditional, IE spirituality is, in my experience, one of the most beautiful, poetic and powerful forms of spiritual practice I have ever experienced. It is my desire to take this noble and beautiful world-view out of the pages of fantasy and into the every day reality of the sincere practitioner. Doing so, in my opinion, has the potential to transform the world into the beautiful, amazing and magical place it has always been.

Thunder Shamans

There are all kinds of shamans; healers, mystics, warriors, sorcerers, poets, etc., There is a very specific kind of shaman who has been called to act as a source of cleansing and evolution. In some cultures, these types of shamans are known for their affinity with the forces of thunder and lightning. This is the kind of shamanism in which I have been trained by my Taoist teachers. And, as a result, I have since focused primarily on the Thunder Path. It is my desire to share this Thunder Path with others who feel a call to participate in cleansing and healing our modern world from the stagnation and destructive effects of modern materialistic, separatist, dualistic thought upon our world.

This is the call of the Thunder Shaman and it is what I share with you here in this book. This book is meant to be an introduction into a life-long practice of cleansing, healing and spiritual evolution which can hopefully be part of the huge energetic shift which has already begun in our Solar System.

The nature of this Energetic shift has already been felt by spiritual workers of all kinds. The actual existence of this shift is not in question. What is in question is whether or not human society will survive this shift. It is certain that those who hold onto the old ways of dualistic thinking will experience major challenges. Those who allow their thinking and actions to adapt to this new holographic model of existence will prosper and evolve.

The challenge for humans is that it is in our nature to perpetuate models of living and thinking which have served us in the past. So, it is very understandable that some people are stubbornly clutching to what they and their parents have known. But, this new spiritual shift that is arriving requires a change in worldview that is aligned with many pre-historic modes of thought. We are being called to reawaken the "Old Ways" while also innovating and evolving new understandings of Spirit. The result is a streamlined, more concentrated approach to ancient ideas.

The challenge of the Thunder Shaman is to act as a conduit of the cleansing power of Thunder and Lightning to help clear away the stagnant energies of the past epoch and help usher humans into this new shift of existence. This shift has arrived and it is up to us to evolve or go the way of the dinosaur. The Thunder Shaman is the adventurer who acts as the doorman to this new dimension. He/she holds open the doorway to Infinity allowing others to walk through safely.

I feel it is my particular calling to uncover the essential aspects of Energy Work and Shamanic Spiritual Science found in traditional spiritual disciplines and distill the most efficient and necessary elements of these practices into a universally applicable practice for the modern Western shaman.

The Thunder Wheel
The main tool I will focus on in this book is what I call the "Thunder Wheel." This is an eight-sided shamanic direction wheel which is used as an energetic compass to orient the shaman to the forces, energies and spirits associated with the nine dimensions of the shamanic Tree of Life or the World Tree.

I have discovered over the years of my practice and research that many of the indigenous shamanic practices of varying cultures from all over the northern hemisphere use a version of the eight-limbed "Medicine Wheel" to orient, summon and channel the forces of Life Force Energy for the purposes of empowerment, healing and ritual.

What was revolutionary for me to discover was the universal applications of the Thunder Wheel in every indigenous spiritual practice that I researched which retained an unbroken connection to their pre-history. I found that after I had interpreted the various cultural and mythological symbolism connected to each of the eight directions on the shamanic direction wheel, that the understanding of the fundamental energies of each direction was identical in each cultural tradition. In regional spiritual practices ranging from Iceland to Southern China that utilized the eight limbed shamanic direction wheel, there existed a universally applicable spiritual science of Life Force Energy that transcended time, distance, language, culture and mythology.

As interesting as all this is, it is not as important to me as the fact that, in my personal experience, the techniques associated with summoning the powers of the eight directions WORKED! I have gone to great lengths to reveal my understanding that the powers of the eight directions were used by many indigenous spiritual traditions but what I have perhaps under stressed is the fact that this is a powerful and effective spiritual science. This stuff really works!

Purpose
The main goal of this book is to introduce the reader to the underlying theory, concepts and practices of the shamanic Thunder Wheel. After reading this book, you will have the necessary tools to understand the mindset of our shamanic ancestors and apply it to our modern world. For those who feel the calling of the Thunder Shaman, they will have the necessary understanding and tools to pursue the advanced practices of Thunder

Shamanism which I will share in upcoming materials (Books, Instructional DVDs, etc.,) related to in-depth techniques for each of the nine spiritual dimensions of the shamanic world tree.

OK, so enough talking, let's get to work...

The Thunder Wheel

In this book, we are going to focus mainly on the eight-limbed shamanic direction wheel which I am calling the Thunder Wheel. In Thunder Shamanism, the Thunder Wheel acts as a compass and also as a gateway through which Life Force Energy can flow, be channeled and directed for spiritual purposes.

(Above: a Thunder Wheel I constructed for personal rituals)

(Bronze Age Eight Sided Stone Circle. Germany)

It is my contention that the eight sided direction wheel is a shamanic tool that has been used by humans since perhaps Paleolithic times. The use of these types of wheels have been documented all over the world. Some noticeable examples are Native American Sacred Hoops or "Medicine Wheels," as well as Stonehenge and other sacred stone circles that are found all over Northern Europe dating back to the Neolithic period.

Viking explorers often wore bronze "sun wheel" brooches on their cloaks. Interestingly enough, Native Hopi tradition teaches that pre-Columbian Hopi shamans knew that European explorers would eventually arrive in the Americas and if the Europeans wore a cross within a circle, that meant that they would remember their shared spiritual connection with Native Americans, but if the Europeans wore crosses with no circle, then that would indicate that Europeans had forgotten their true spiritual heritage and would bring disaster to Native Americans.

As it happened, The first European explorers wore the Christian cross which is the cross with no circle and we all know what happened after that... One can only imagine if Europe had not abandoned her indigenous spiritual values if perhaps Norse pagan explorers wearing the bronze Sun Wheel would have been the first Europeans to contact the Native Americans and how differently things may have unfolded. We'll never know...

Bronze Age "sunwheel" brooches, found in Zurich, Switzerland

The more we discover about our pre-Christian European past, we discover more and more about our intimate spiritual connection with various forms of the wheel.

The eight limbed wheel is still used to this day in various indigenous spiritual disciplines which retain their pre-historic connections.

The Thunder Wheel and the Directions

Each of the eight directions projects a particular vibration of Life Force Energy which is transmitted into the center of the wheel. The center represents manifested physical reality where all humans reside.

The eight directions plus the center equals the number nine. This is the number of spiritual dimensions or "worlds" associated with the shamanic World Tree or the Tree of Life.

The Number Nine
The most widespread model of the shamanic world tree in various indigenous traditions contains nine branches or nine worlds. Coincidentally, the human body has nine chakras. (Most people are familiar with the seven main chakras associated with Vedic/Hindu Yogic mysticism, but in esoteric Yogic sciences there are actually nine chakras). Taoist mysticism ascribes nine main energetic points on the trunk of the body which correspond approximately to the nine chakras in esoteric yogic mysticism.

In popular neo-shamanism that focuses on visionary journeys there are "three worlds" of Upper, Middle and Lower which correspond respectively with superconscious, conscious and subconscious realms. This type of neo-shamanism that uses hypnotic drums to facilitate visionary journeying is based largely on traditional Siberian Shamanism (Tengerism).

However, it is not as well known that in the Tengerist cosmology, there are actually nine branches on the World Tree not just the three worlds of neo-shamanism. According to one source I discovered, Siberian

Shamans during initiation would climb a tree while simultaneously in a hypnotic visionary state, imagine themselves climbing up through all nine branches of the World Tree. After reaching the final branch, the initiate would literally fall from the tree and be caught by assistants below. The actual fall from the tree symbolized the shaman "falling into" the shamanic spiritual reality thereby enabling him to enter the spiritual realm at will.

As with the Siberian World Tree, there are nine "Worlds" or spiritual dimensions on the pre-Christian Norse World Tree. In Norse mythology, the god Odin (Fury of Self-Awareness) hangs himself on the trunk of the World Tree for nine nights and receives complete enlightenment (self-awareness). At the end of his nine-day ordeal, Odin is given a vision of the Runes (spiritual mysteries) and like the Siberian example, Odin falls from the tree after receiving his vision. The result of his shamanic initiation earns him the title of "All Father" and is recognized as leader of the celestial gods.

These nine spiritual dimensions of the direction wheel carry specific energies which are mirrored in the nine main energetic points (chakras) of the body. The human body can be seen as a microcosm of the infinite cosmos. Simultaneously, the nine points of the human body can be seen as nine points of reception and accumulation where the vibrations of the nine spiritual dimensions are stored and projected from the human body.

As I mentioned in the introduction, according to my research, while different cultures use different symbolism for each of the eight directions, once the symbolic meanings have been decoded and translated, we find that in many ancient traditions, the qualities of each direction are the same.

Here are some of the possible universal interpretations of the qualities of each of the nine worlds/directions of the Thunder Wheel as found in multiple indigenous spiritual traditions:

The Nine Worlds

1) North "Waters Of Life"
Water Element, Waters of Life, Waters of Creation, Nurturing, The Planet Mercury, Unmanifest Potential, Mists of Creation, The Void, Conception of Life, The Base Chakra

2) NorthEast "Fort of the Gods"
Highest Aether, Highest Heaven, Realm of the Celestial Gods, The Planet Jupiter, Morals, Integrity, Worship, Dharma, "Spiritual But Not Religious," Temples, Sacred Space, Altars, Universality, Neutrality, Pacifism, Life Purpose, The Superconscious, The Crown Chakra

3) East "Thunder/Life Force"
Aether Element, Thunder, Lightning, Thunder Gods, Primordial Giants, Laws of Physics, Trolls, The Sun, Life Force Energy, Physical Power, The Soul, Protection from Evil, Individuality, Ego, The Sexual Chakra

4) SouthEast "Home of Magical Powers"
The Human Mind, Mental Powers, Magic, Ritual, Talismans, Writing, Prayer, Mantras, Charms, Spells,

Dwarves, Emotions, Internal Spiritual Fire, Kundalini, The Planet Venus, Manifestation of Intention, The Subconscious, Third Eye Chakra

5) **South "Realm of Primordial Fire"** The Fire Element, Destruction, Transformation, Success, Emotional and Artistic Expression, Entropy, Spontaneity, The Planet Mars, Domination, War, Death, Navel Chakra

6) **SouthWest "The Underworld"**
Hell, Reincarnation, Karmic Attachments, Karmic Debts, Web of Wyrd, Past Lives, Limbo, Shamanic Journeys, Immediate Ethnic Ancestors, North Node of The Moon, Demon Possession, Nightmares, Unfulfilled Desires, Lasting Effects of Spoken Words, The Unconscious, The Tongue and Mouth meridian (Yes, the mouth is also a powerful meridian or chakra.)

7) **West "Land of Plenty"**
The Air Element, Experience, Fertility Gods, Nature Spirits, Sprites, Fairies, Time, The Ocean, Law, Karmic Justice, Meditation, Psychic Powers, Shapeshifting, Astral Travel, Solar Plexus ,The Planet Saturn, Patience, Old Age, Wisdom, The Solar Plexus Chakra (not to be confused with the heart or navel)

8) **NorthWest "Gateway to Infinity"**
Clouds, Ascended Masters, Mentorship, Akashic Records, Spiritual Mastery, Teaching, The Moon, Divine Speech, Prophecy, Channeling of Higher Voices, Near Death/Out of Body Travels, Ancient/Original Ancestors, Elves, Higher Self, Ultimate Enlightenment, Spiritual Liberation from Incarnation, Throat Chakra

9) Center "Earth"

Earth Element, Manifested Reality, Three Dimensional Existence, Middle Earth, Plants, Animals, Soil, Food, Grounding, Gravity, The Planet Earth, The Heart Chakra

The number nine is widely recognized in both modern and ancient spiritual paths as being the number of completion, transformation, etc., There is no accident that the world tree, the human body and the shamanic direction wheel all culminate in the number nine.

13th century SunWheel, Temple of Konark, Orissa, India

Indo-European Mythology And The Creation Myths

The Creation Mythology of the Pre-Christian Norse people and the ancient Vedic tribes of India have striking similarities which cannot be ignored. While there are some notable differences, we can see a very clear proto Indo-European source mythology for the creation of the Cosmos from which both of these traditions arose.

What this indicates to me is that both the Vedic and Norse traditions are very possibly derived from a pre-historic, proto-Indo European root tradition that stretches back perhaps 50,000 years to the first proto-Indo European settlers of the Northern Hemisphere.

According to pre-Christian Norse mythology, the Cosmos existed in emptiness and had no definition. Over time, the void of pre-creation began to separate into two Primordial Realms of Fire and Water. These "Worlds" were called the "Home of Mist" (Nifleheim) located in the North and the "Home of Fire" (Muspelheim) located in the South. In the center was a vast and frightening, vacuum-filled void full of raw, unmanifested potential called "The Yawning Chasm" (Ginnungagap).

Sparks of Primordial Fire from the Fire Home and drops of Primordial Water from the Mist Home were slowly sucked into the Yawning Chasm. Sparks of the Primordial Fire and drops of Primordial Water began to coalesce and interact creating the first being, an immense giant named "Ymir."

"Ymir" in Old Norse language is etymologically related to the name of the Vedic god of death called "Yama" in Sanskrit. Yama is known as the first person to die, because he was the first being in the cosmos to die, he therefore was given mastery over death. Ymir in Norse Mythology is also the first being to "die" when he was dismembered by the gods Odin, Villi and Ve and his body used to create the physical, manifested cosmos.

The words Ymir and Yama come from the proto Indo-European word "Yemos" which means "Twin." The dual (twin) aspect of Ymir is revealed when, his two feet mate with each other to create a "many headed" giant from which the race of giants are born.

Out of his armpits, Ymir sweats out the primordial essences of male and female or as the Taoists would call them, the forces of Yin (female) and Yang (male). The twin or mirror effect is seen in that out of Ymir's left armpit comes the masculine essence and out of his right armpit comes the feminine essence. In manifested reality, this polarity is reversed as Right is Masculine and Left is Feminine.

This is significant because the right side of the human body is associated with the left brain, the discerning faculty (Masculine) and the left side of the body is associated with the right brain, the Intuitive, (Feminine). But, in Ymir's body, we see a mirror (twin) reflection of how masculine and feminine are manifested in the Cosmos. In Ymir's body, the left side is masculine and the right side is feminine. Or, perhaps it is we who are the mirrored reflection of the primordial. In either case, we see another aspect of Ymir's dual nature.

Meanwhile, out of the primordial "ice" (concentrated potential) there arose the Cow of Sustenance named "Audumbla." Ymir suckled primordial "milk" from Audumbla's teets. While Ymir was suckling the milk from Audumbla, she herself was licking from a salty block of ice which revealed the first of the primordial deities to arise named "Buri" (The Producer).

Buri gave birth to the celestial deities know as the "Aesir." The word "Aesir" is etymologically related to the Indo-European words "Ahura" (Avestian/Persian) and "Asura" (Sanskrit). All of these words can be translated into "Being of Power." The Hindus have associated the Asuras with the Earthly deities similar to the Vanir of Norse Mythology while the Devas have been associated with the Celestial deities. But, originally, in Vedic times, the word Asura was used for any deity whether they be Earthly or Celestial. The Devas were simply a subset of the Asuras. The Norse language retains the original

Indo-European root meaning of the word reflected in the word Aesir (Celestial Deities).

The Old Norse word "Buri" (Producer) is related to the Sanskrit word "Brahma" which is the Vedic god of creation who "produces" all of manifested creation.

Buri had three grandsons named "Furious Awareness" (Odin), "Willpower" (Villi) and "Sacred Space" (Ve). These Celestial "brothers" engaged Ymir in battle and slew him. These three deities then dismembered Ymir's corpse and used it to create and delineate all of physical, manifested reality. Ymir's blood became the oceans, his bones became the mountains, his hair became the trees, his brains became the clouds.

Odin, Villi and Ve are specifically associated with human awareness. It is these three deities who gave the first humans their Life (Odin), Spirit (Villi) and Awareness (Ve).

What this part of the Norse myth is saying is that the three human faculties of Awareness, Intent and Perception delineate and create our visible universe where we live. Without the three properties of Awareness, Intent and Perception we humans would not be able to perceive or experience three dimensional reality.

Vedic mythology portrays a very similar version of the Creation myth. The 4,000 year old Rig Veda also speaks of a titanic being called the "Purusha" who is "sacrificed" by the Celestial gods in order to create the manifested Cosmos.

"When they divided the Purusha, into how many parts did they disperse him?... The moon was born from his mind; the sun was born from his eye... From his navel the atmosphere was born; from his head the heaven appeared. From his two feet came the earth, and the regions of the sky from his ear. Thus they (the Celestial gods) fashioned the worlds...when the gods, spreading

the sacrifice, bound down the Purusha as the sacrificial beast."

The War Between Giants And Gods In Norse Mythology

It is important to define the difference between the Giants (Jotuns) and the Celestial Deities (Aesir). The Giants represent the titanic forces of the laws of macro scale physics (Gravity, Time, Entropy, etc…) These forces have very little awareness of tiny beings like humans. These are the Titans of Greek mythology. They are perceived by us as being aggressive toward humans, but in reality, the Giants are just massive forces of Nature that are following their inherent natures and are not necessarily seeking to harm us. The Celestial Deities, on the other hand, are closely linked to conscious awareness and have a vested interest in the formation and protection of all conscious life. So, the Aesir have an agenda to promote, protect and extend conscious existence. When conscious life comes into conflict with the laws of physics, the Aesir seek to "battle" the destructive forces of the Universe that tend to work against life.

A good example of the gods battling the forces of physics is exemplified in the deity of lightning and thunder. And since we are seeking to learn Thunder Shamanism it is appropriate that we look at how the Forces of Thunder protect life. The Vedic version of the Thunder god is Indra, the Norse version is Thor. In physics, the Thunder god is represented as the Electro-Magnetic Force. Vedic mythology says that the Sun sits in the East and worships Indra for "long life." As it so happens, inside the sun, the massive gravity inside its core crushes hydrogen molecules fusing them together. This nuclear fusion results in the explosive energy of heat and light.

However, the ElectroMagnetic Force is 1,000,000,000,000,000,000,000,000,000,000,000,000 times stronger than the force of gravity. It can't stop gravity, but it slows it down. The result is that the Sun would burn itself out much more quickly without the ElectroMagnetic Force to slow down the process of nuclear fusion. So, in a very real sense, the Vedic shamans were correct when they observed that it is the power of Electromagnetism that gives long life to the Sun. As in the mythology, the god of Electromagnetism works tirelessly to protect the source of all nourishment (Sun) from the destructive influence of the titanic force of Gravity

In Norse mythology, Thor is constantly off in the East (Giant Home) fighting the giants and protecting both the gods and humans from their destructive effects. The talismanic symbol for Thor is the Thurisaz Rune which is a Rune of protection. Thor protects humans and drives away destructive forces from them. Similarly, the ElectroMagnetic field creates a tiny but impenetrable barrier between molecules. This invisible barrier is what keeps me from sinking through my chair as I write this and being pulled to the center of the Earth and crushed by gravity. Thor is said to be the protector of the gods, the Realm of Midgard and, specifically of humans. He fights against gravity, Old Age and Time. In a very real sense this is true. Everything we interact with in three dimensional reality is encased and protected by the ElectroMagnetic Field. In this way, Thor is constantly fighting against the giants. He never completely defeats them, but without him, we would be annihilated by the sheer force of the effects of Gravity, Time, Old Age, Decay, etc,. This power to protect conscious life is what we Thunder Shamans seek to promote and channel through our spiritual work.

There are two types of Giants in Norse Mythology; the Jotuns (pronounced "Yo-tons") and the Trolls. The Jotuns, we have already discussed. The Trolls are like mini jotuns who are aggressive and destructive to humans. These are the giant beings of fairy tales that go around stomping through villages, taking people hostage, killing and eating people, etc… These beings represent mindless, unconscious expansion of life force. Aggressive, narcissistic people who cause havoc in other peoples' lives without taking responsibility for their actions are acting from their "troll" nature.

The gods have declared an ongoing state of war against the trolls. This "battle" represents the forces of conscious evolution struggling against the forces of chaos within the human beings. It is like the battle of our frontal cortex as it seeks to evolve beyond our "reptilian" brain stem. By seeking the aid of the celestial deities, we are more able to gain control of our baser instincts and strive for higher spiritual evolution.

Dwarves - Masters of Magic
According to Norse mythology, out of the leftover ambient Life Force Energy found in Ymir's blood, the Celestial gods created "humanoid" beings which laid the foundation for the essence of all psychological and

emotional awareness. These "humanoid" beings of Life Force Energy create the infrastructure of emotional and psychological patterns of all conscious, incarnated life. These beings have the power to channel Life Force Energy into emotions and use this power to create matter. These beings are masters of creating and manifesting with their intent through Life Force Energy. These beings are the first masters of Magic. These beings were called "Dwarves" in Norse mythology.

The Dwarves are relevant to the Thunder Wheel because the four Cardinal Directions of North, South, East and West are names of Dwarves created by the Celestial Deities when mapping out the Cosmos. This indicates that the cardinal directions are conscious, magical entities.

Dwarves are also important to shamans because all human psychological and emotional patterns are derived from the emotional and psychological infrastructure created by the first Dwarves. Many of the names of the first Dwarves are names of human emotions and psychological traits. A few Dwarf names are: *Magician, Yearning, Longing, Wisdom, Hope and Will.*

Remember that Dwarves are nothing more than beings of pure Life Force Energy which were fashioned into "humanoid" form by the Celestial Gods. They were not human but human*oid*. They were the molds through which human emotional and psychological patterns are given to incarnated people. Humans are infinite, eternal, souls who have, at their core, the essence of the Celestial deities. The word "Soul" is derived from the Anglo-Saxon word "Sawul" which literally means "Sun."

Our souls are little "suns." Human beings are stars encased in flesh. In order to be incarnated as humans, we need to superimpose emotional and psychological patterns onto our soul-consciousness in order to better interface with material reality. Without this power of the Dwarves imposed upon our soul-awareness, we would have no desires and, in effect, we would sit around all day lost in the bliss of our Divine, Celestial essence desiring nothing and doing nothing. The desires, emotions and psychological patterns given to us by our humanoid, Dwarf natures allow us to strive, to interact and to create our three dimensional lives.

This means that it is through channeling the Life Force Energy of our human emotions with the power of desire focused by intent that we humans create our reality. In order to truly understand the power of magic and shamanism, one must first become a human.

If you are called to be a shaman, one main reason you incarnated into physical life was so that you could experience human emotions and learn to master them. Because it is only through the focusing of Life Force Energy channeled by intent fueled by emotions that shamans, sorcerers and magicians can effect change in the physical world.

Coincidentally, the Old English word for Sorcery was "Dvergamal" which means "Dwarf Speak." Does this word mean that a sorcerer creates magic by speaking his commands to Dwarves who fulfill his wishes? Or, does it mean that the sorcerer understands the secret language of Dwarves and cooperates with them to manipulate reality? Either way, Dwarves apparently play an important role in magic and shamanism.

The Four Cardinal Directions in Norse Myth
OK, so back to the Creation myth and its relevance to the Thunder Wheel… Remember, we are told that:

North is the realm of primordial Waters
and
South is the realm of primordial Fire.

So, What about East and West?

Jotunheim (Giant Home) East
We are told of a primordial forest called "Ironwood" deep within Giant Home, East of Midgard (Middle Earth).

Vanaheim (Wanes' Home) West
Besides the Celestial gods (Aesir), Norse mythology also prominently features the "elder" gods of Fertility known as the "Vanir." The Vanir live in the West in a place called "Vanaheim."

Midgard (Middle Earth) Center
In the center of these worlds is the "Middle Yard" (Midgard/Middle Earth) where humans live.

Placement of the Psychological Realms
Norse mythology is very clear about the location of these first five worlds which compose the Five Realms of North, South, East, West and Center within the Cardinal Wheel (Celtic Cross). Since the realms of the Cardinal Wheel have a strong correlation to manifested,

physical reality, it makes sense that Norse mythology would clearly state their physical location.

The other four worlds or Psychological Realms are not clearly stated in Norse mythology. Since these realms have less correlation with physical, manifested reality, it makes sense that there would be less need to state a physical location for their placement.

So, how can we deduce the physical placement of the four Realms of the Psychological Wheel? These remaining four Worlds in Norse Mythology are known as:

"Asgard" (Fort Of The Gods),
"LjossAlfheim" (Light-Elf Home/Ethereal Masters),
"Helheim" (Hel Home/Underworld)
and
"SvartAlfheim" (Dark-Elf Home or Dwarf Home/
Subconscious Forces).

Norse Psychological Worlds

While Norse mythology does not directly state the placement of the Psychological realms in terms of a direction wheel, we can easily deduce their locations by determining the corresponding energetic qualities of these directions found within both the Indo-European Vedic Dig Chakra (Direction Wheel) and with the Taoist BaGua (Eight Gates). (Note that the Ba Gua is inversed with South at the top and North at the bottom.

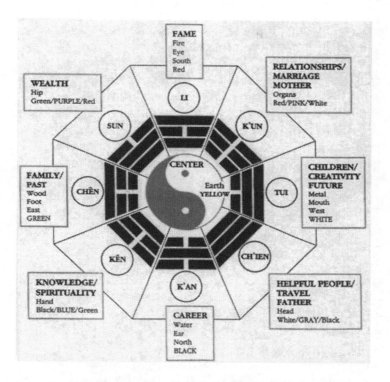

FAME
Fire
Eye
South
Red

RELATIONSHIPS/ MARRIAGE MOTHER
Organs
Red/PINK/White

WEALTH
Hip
Green/PURPLE/Red

LI

SUN

K'UN

FAMILY/ PAST
Wood
Foot
East
GREEN

CHÊN

CENTER

Earth
YELLOW

TUI

CHILDREN/ CREATIVITY FUTURE
Metal
Mouth
West
WHITE

KÊN

CH'IEN

KNOWLEDGE/ SPIRITUALITY
Hand
Black/BLUE/Green

K'AN

HELPFUL PEOPLE/ TRAVEL FATHER
Head
White/GRAY/Black

CAREER
Water
Ear
North
BLACK

The ancient, indigenous shamanic path of China is Taoism. The Taoists use the eight sided direction wheel perhaps more than any other tradition on the planet. It is used for Shamanic Ritual, Feng Shui, Medicine, Martial Arts and more. While the Taoist tradition is not Indo-European in nature, they share the same understanding of the nature of the eight directions as do the indigenous Indo-European shamanic traditions. If the similarity between the Norse and the Vedic traditions wasn't enough, comparing them to the Taoist tradition will add even more credibility to the understanding that the qualities of the eight-sided shamanic direction wheel is an objective spiritual science and is not limited to cultural or ethnic peculiarities.

The Diagonal "Psychological" directions in the Ba Gua
In the Taoist Post-Heaven BaGua symbol, The NorthEast "Ken" is the Realm of "Mountain" which vibrates with the highest Spirituality. The SouthWest is the Realm of Deepest Earth "Kun" and resonates with the forces of "Mother" and re-birth. The NorthWest "Ch'ien" is the Realm of "Heaven" which resonates with mentors and helpful advice. The SouthEast "Sun" is "Wind" and is often referred to as the "Human Door" which resonates prosperity, wealth and abundance as well as the properties of the human subconscious.

When we compare the placement of energetic qualities in the diagonal "gates" of the BaGua with the Norse Psychological Worlds of the World Tree, The correlation seems clear.

The ethereal realm of "Mountain" in the NorthWest is strikingly similar to the Norse world of "Asgard." The NorthWestern realm of "Heaven" from where the "helpful advice" of the enlightened ones emanates is reminiscent of the Norse Realm of the Ascended Masters (Elves) of the Light Elf Home. The Realm of Deepest Earth in the SouthWest correlates with Hel Home (Underworld). "The Human Door" in the SouthEast corresponds with the Norse "Dwarf Home" (Realm of the Subconscious).

Vedic Deity Placement on the Thunder Wheel
Now let's look at the placement of deities in the Vedic Astrological Direction Wheel (Dig Chakra) so we can compare their understanding of the energetic qualities of directions with both the Taoist Ba Gua and the Norse direction wheel.

Vedic Deity Wheel

North - Kubera - Mercury
Kubera is the god of riches. In this case, riches can be likened to resource potential.

NorthEast - Ishana Shiva - Jupiter
Ishana means "ruler." In this case it refers to the highest spiritual principle and the Ruler of the gods.

East - Indra - Sun
Indra is the god of lightning and thunder, the Force of ElectroMagnetism, the first principle of Life Force Energy.

SouthEast - Agni - Venus
Agni is the Vedic god who is lord of the Spiritual Fire used in sacrifices that carries the smoke (prayers/meditation) of human sacrifices to the heavens.

South - Yama - Mars
Yama is the god of "death" or transformation.

SouthWest - Niruti - North Node
Niruti is a Demoness of the Underworld

West - Varuna - Saturn
Varuna is the Vedic god of the Waters of Fertility

NorthWest - Vayu - Moon
Vayu is the god of the Air (Atmosphere/Sky)

IE Planetary Wheel

North is lorded by the god Kubera, the god of riches and the planet Mercury. In the Vedic understanding, riches are derived from the accumulation of potential resources. The Ba Gua represents the North as the realm of Successful Career. Although the cultural symbolism is slightly different between the Vedic and Taoist understandings, The Norse version bridges the gap where the Element of Water is clearly attested to in Norse Mythology as residing in the Northern Direction. This is in complete agreement with the Taoist placement of the Water Element.

The NorthEast is lorded by the god Ishana Shiva, the Ruler of the Gods and the planet Jupiter. Vedic myth says he resides on top of Mount Kailash. The correlation to the Taoist ethereal NorthEastern realm of "mountain" is undeniable. If the Norse realm of Asgard where the "AllFather" Odin sits on his divine throne is compared with the Vedic and Taoist versions of the qualities of the NorthEastern Direction, there is only one logical direction for the placement of Asgard - The NorthEast.

The East is lorded by the god Indra and the Sun. Indra is the god of Thunder and Lightning. The Taoists often refer to the East as the realm of "Thunder." The Norse mythological tradition associates the Eastern Realm with the thunder god Thor, the half-god, half-giant who constantly battles with the giants in the East. So, there is no argument here. Deities of Lightning and Thunder reside in the East.

The SouthEastern Realm is lorded by Agni, the Vedic god of sacrificial Fire and the planet Venus. Agni is not to be confused solely with physical fire. In proto-Indo European languages, there were always two words for Fire. One word 'Pyr' (English 'Fire') was the external, physical force of Fire. The second word for fire (now mostly forgotten in modern Indo-European languages) was the internal, spiritual force of fire (*'Agni' - Sanskrit, 'Igni' - Greek and Latin, 'Ing' - Proto Germanic*). It is this spiritual fire which is directly connected to fire sacrifices performed by humans which allow them to receive divine inspiration to achieve their highest potential. In yogic meditation, the internal spiritual fire is known as Kundalini which is associated with human spiritual awakening of the latent human potential. In the Norse tradition, it is the uniquely human aspect of the Dwarf Nature that allows them to achieve the "human" state. The Taoist tradition calls this direction "The Human Door." While the associations may be somewhat unclear on a superficial comparison, the underlying connections seem to agree that the best placement for the Norse world of the "Dwarf Home" is in the SouthEast.

The Vedic god lording the Southern direction is Yama, the god of death. The planet associated with this direction is Mars, the planet of War and Death who is associated with the Element of Fire. The Norse Mythology is very clear that the South is the Realm of Fire.

The Planet associated with the SouthWest is the North Node of the moon named Rahu who is the head of a decapitated dragon. The Vedic goddess lording the SouthWestern Direction is Niruti who is a demoness of the underworld representing the unconscious human attachments that must be released in order to attain liberation from the cycle of death and re-birth. The Taoists see this direction as the realm of the deepest Earth and of the motherly influence. In Norse tradition, the underworld is guarded by the goddess Hella who is daughter of the god Loki. She combines the essence of the both the Taoist and Vedic versions by integrating a Goddess of the underworld ('demon') with the deepest Earthly form of the Mother, (a nurturing Feminine deity who assists in re-birth.) So, the only logical location for the Norse underworld of Hel is the SouthWest.

The West is lorded by the planet Saturn. The Vedic god of the West is named Varuna, the god of the Waters of the Ocean. The Norse tradition is clear about the Western realm which is lorded by the god of the Ocean who is named 'Njord'. Njord is classified as a member of the Vanir, the earthly gods of fertility who often fight with the celestial gods. The Vanir are clearly located in the

West in Norse mythology. So, the Realm of Vanaheim in the West is quite clear.

The Vedic god of the Northwest is Vayu, the god of Wind. The planet associated with this Direction is the Moon. The Taoists associate this direction with "Helpful Advice." The Moon is understood to be symbolic of the highest reflection of the Divine Human Mind. If the SouthEast is the Realm of the essence of the Human Mind and the NorthWest is the realm of "helpful advice" and the Divine Mind, then the only logical placement for the Norse world of the Light Elves is in the NorthWest.

The Center is representative of the Earth, meaning the Earth upon which we stand, so, the Norse World of "Middle Earth" can be in no other location than in the middle of the Thunder Wheel, the center…

It may be slightly difficult, at first, to see the correlations to the Psychological realms, but if we peer beneath the veneer of superficial mythological symbolism in these different cultures, the underlying energies of each of the directions becomes clear. It is just too coincidental, in my opinion, for these three, very ancient and different ethnic, linguistic and cultural traditions to have essentially the same understanding about the energetic qualities of each direction.

The fact that, under the surface, these mythological definitions correlate with each other, indicates that this common understanding about the quality of energies in these directions is a result of objective observation. In other words, this is a spiritual science that reflects objective laws of Life Force Energy that can be observed by anyone who is without personal agenda and has the ability to objectively discern Spiritual Energies.

If there is this degree of agreement among these culturally diverse traditions in terms of the energetic qualities of all nine realms, then we can safely deduce that there exists an objective spiritual science of Life Force Energy as reflected in the eight-sided shamanic direction wheel.

Since the qualities of the directions in the Taoist, Vedic and Norse traditions all share striking similarities, then I think we will have discovered a universally applicable medicine wheel which seems to reflect objective laws of Life Force Energy as expressed in the eight directions and the nine worlds of the World Tree which can be accessed by anyone of any culture or time period.

Re-Constructed Norse World Tree Direction Wheel
Based on my personal experience working with the eight directions and the nine worlds, combined with my research into other shamanic direction wheels I have constructed this wheel for placement of the Nine Worlds of the Norse World Tree. Understanding the nature of the directions is helpful when channeling different energies from the directions.

The Nine Worlds of The Norse World Tree

North - Mist Home
NorthEast - Asgard (Fort of the Gods)
East - Giant Home
SouthEast - Dwarf Home
South - Fire Home
SouthWest - Hel Home
West - Wanes Home
NorthWest - Elf Home
Center - Midgard (Middle Earth)

There is a difference, however, between summoning energies into our world and actually journeying to the source of the directions for interaction with the deities and spirits of the directions. When one wants to journey to the source of the directions, it is helpful to understand the nature of the beings and entities who reside in each dimension.

To this end, I have found the Norse mythological symbolism of the Nine Worlds and of the entities therein to be, for me, the most potent for my imagination to hold on to. Whether that is just my personal bias or not, using the symbolism of Norse World Tree Direction Wheel in shamanic ritual works extremely well for me.

It is interesting to observe the increasing popularity of pre-Christian Indo-European spirituality all around the world in the forms of Fantasy and Science Fiction movies, books and video games (which get the majority of their symbology directly from pre-Christian Norse mythology).

Archetypal characters such as Wizards, Elves, Dwarves, Trolls etc., hold an increasingly more powerful place in the subconscious fantasies of more and more people all over the world. As such, this imagery and symbolism interact very well with the modern Western subconscious mind. In my experience, when the subconscious mind is happy, shamanic work is extremely effective and fruitful. So, using imagery and symbolism that excites the subconscious mind will result in more powerful results in our spiritual work.

Modern media has created a scenario where after a one thousand year period of obscurity, the ancient shamanic wisdom of the Northern European people has the potential to awaken a renewed shamanic understanding of the Cosmos that can potentially be accessed by anyone within modern society regardless of cultural or ethnic background.

So, for those wanting a more universally applicable Thunder Wheel who are not inclined to follow a particular ethnic path, the forces of the Nine Realms of the Tree of Life can be summed up in this fashion:

North: Forces of Creation/Potential
NorthEast: Celestial Gods/Superconscious
East: Thunder/Giants
SouthEast: Magic/Human Subconscious
South: Destruction/Transformation
SouthWest: UnderWorld/Unconscious Forces
West: Nature Spirits/Fertility
NorthWest: Ascended Masters/ Higher Self
Center: Three-Dimensional Manifested Reality

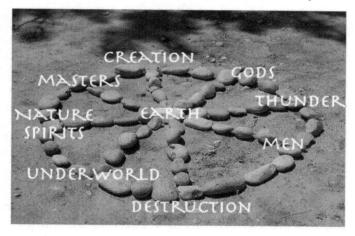

Of course, the Shaman is free to use whatever symbolism works best for them to symbolize these forces. Understanding the basics of this Thunder Wheel system on an intuitive level, the shaman can create a Thunder Wheel for whatever purpose they choose.

OK, so by now you should have a pretty good idea of the nature of each of the directions on the Thunder Wheel. Feel free to review this chapter on a regular basis and meditate on the different cultural symbology of the directions. In my experience, understanding how these different cultures viewed the directions will create a deeper and more detailed tapestry of the how the Energies of the different directions interact.

But, wait, there's more!... Now, we are going to look at the Five Elements and their placement on the direction wheel. One of the first things a Thunder Shaman needs to do is to learn how to channel and absorb the powers of the Five Elements.

The Five Elements of Vedic, Taoist and Norse Direction Wheels

In terms of locations of the Elemental Powers, the Taoist, Vedic and Norse direction wheels are in complete agreement. Water is in the North, Fire is in the South, Aether/Wood is in the East, Air/Metal is in the West and Earth is in the Center.

(Note: Taoism calls Aether "Wood" and Air "Metal." Apart from that difference, the qualities of each of the Five Elements in both Vedic and Taoist traditions is identical.)

If you know where to look and with a little sleuthing, the Norse tradition does reveal which directions the Five Elements reside. This evidence will confirm exactly with what we find in both the Taoist and Vedic traditions for the locations of the Elements.

North (Water) and South (Fire)
We have already observed in Norse Creation mythology that the Realm of the Primordial Waters is in the North and the Primordial World of Fire is in the South which agrees exactly with both Taoist and Vedic sources.

East (Aether/Wood - Thunder)
The Eastern Realm is the home of the Giants who can represent the power of expansion of Life Force Energy. This would agree with the placement of Aether/Wood Element in the East which represents expansion of Spirit Energy/Life Force Energy.

In Vedic astrological teaching, the Eastern direction is lorded by Indra, the god of Lightning, Thunder and Life Force Energy. In Taoism, the East is the realm of the Green Dragon and of Thunder. It is quite the coincidence that both Vedic and Taoist sources specifically use the word for Thunder to describe the Energy located here and place it in the East.

In the Norse tradition, Thor, the god of lightning and thunder is often away on journeys in the East as he fights off the giants. So, in each of these traditions, the Eastern direction has a direct correlation with the powers of Lightning and Thunder.

West (Air/Metal)
Vedic and Taoist traditions place Air/Metal in the West. In the Norse tradition, West is the home of the Vanir who are often described as masters of Wind (Air) in the Norse mythological lore.

In the Norse mythological tale called "Alvismal" a Dwarf named "Allwise" describes to Thor how the different entities (Gods, Giants, Vanir, Humans, etc.,) describe the various aspects of manifested reality. In the case of the Vanir, they almost always describe various natural phenomena in the context of Wind. For example, the Vanir refer to Clouds as "Wind Rivers" and the Sky as "Wind Maker."

When asked about the Wind itself, the Vanir call it "Neigher" meaning a horse that neighs. This indicates that the Vanir ride on top of the Wind as a human would ride a horse. So, the best placement for the Air Element according to Norse mythology would be in the West with the masters of Wind, the Vanir.

Center (Earth)

So, then, in terms of the locations of the Five Elements, we have complete agreement in the Norse, Taoist and Vedic traditions.

Five Element Wheel

The Elements are very important to shamanic work. The Thunder Shaman can use the Elements for healing or for cleansing. The shaman can send energy to those who need physical, spiritual and emotional healing. He/She can also send the elements to cleanse or drive away negative energy in spiritual warfare. But first, the shaman needs to absorb the Elements in his/her body. In any case, mastery of the Five Elements is essential to mastery of Life Force Energy.

Five Manifestations of Life Force Energy

There is only one Universal Life Force Energy that creates the physical Cosmos. However, that Energy subdivides itself and "moves" in Five different ways. The

Cosmos is not static, it is constantly in fluid motion creating, maintaining and dissolving. When we observe Life Force Energy moving in one of these five different ways, we call each movement an "Element." But these Elements are not stationary, they are just apexes of movement in a much larger, fluid cycle. The five movements of Life Force Energy are:

Expanding (Aether)
Contracting (Air)
Rising (Fire)
Falling (Water)
Centering (Earth)

It is also how Life Force Energy manifests as it gains greater density. Ether is the least dense and Earth is the most dense. As newly formed Life Force Energy achieves separation from the unmanifest Void, it becomes Aether and as it gains more density and mass, it transforms to Air, then Fire, then Water, then Earth.

In Taoism, this progression of Elements is called the "Destructive Cycle." I call this progression, the Cleansing Cycle. This is summoning Life Force Energy from the purest, pre-manifestation stage when the Life Energy is most potent. This is Life Force Energy emerging directly from the Void. It has a cleansing effect because it tends to destroy stagnant energy. For entities that are operating destructively, this purest of Life Force Energy will either destroy the negativity or transform it to a more benevolent state. This is the power of Thunder and of the god of Thunder who protects and cleanses planet Earth. Think of the feeling in the air after a powerful lightning strike. This is the power of the Cleansing Cycle what I also refer to as "Calling The Storm."

Cleansing Cycle
Aether-Air-Fire-Water-Earth

The other progression of Elements used in Thunder Shamanism is what the Taoists call the "Creative Cycle." I also refer to it as the "Gathering Cycle." This is the gathering of Elemental Life Force Energy after it has been manifested. This cycle is used for healing, relaxation and meditation.

Gathering Cycle
Aether-Fire-Earth-Air-Water

In this cycle, the Elements feed each other to create more energy which can be stored for later use. Aether fuels Fire which releases the Energy trapped in plant material. The ashes from the Fire nourish the soil of Earth. As the Essence of these absorbed nutrients is released into the atmosphere (Air) through evaporation, it forms into clouds and returns the nutrients to the soil as rain (Water).

There are more progressions, but these two have been most helpful in my personal work. Especially the Cleansing Cycle because it is the power of Thunder which I have been called to use to help cleanse and protect.

A note of caution: These Elemental progressions are not theoretical. They are very real. If you call forth the Elements in the ways I will share with you, you WILL experience and feel the power of the Elements in your body. The Elements are extremely powerful and reactive. If someone plays with them without proper training and protocol or attempts to mix them together improperly or out of sequence, it can have disastrous results. I have personally witnessed the negative consequences of those who have disrespectfully played around with the Elements. From personal experience and observation, I do not recommend experimenting with the Elements without proper instruction and guidance.

Part of the problem with teaching high level shamanic techniques through books is the very real possibility for misunderstanding and improper execution which can have destructive results. I will be sharing here a safe and powerful way to work with the Elements. There are however, many other, extremely powerful techniques for summoning and channeling the Elements which involve, breath, movement, visualization, chanting, etc., but I only teach those methods to apprentices whom I can safely monitor. But for now, I will happily share one very powerful and safe fundamental method of working with the Elements which, if practiced regularly, can serve the shaman for a lifetime.

Five Element Breathing Exercises

The Thunder Shaman should have the ability to call the Elements to him/herself whenever he/she chooses to do so. One of the simplest and most effective methods is called the "Five Element Breaths." The original method of the Five Element Breaths was written down by a Shang Ch'ing Taoist master named Tao Hong Jing almost 1500 years ago. He left very clear instructions on silently whispering the Five Element sounds as "breaths." They were never meant to be voiced.

Over time, the original whispering technique has become altered by many Taoist teachers and in some instances, its original power has been watered down as a result. Many Taoist masters, to this day refer to this exercise as the "Five Element Sounds" and teach people to voice these sounds aloud. This is a deviation from the original method.

But, I will teach you here the original method for summoning the Five Elements written down 1500 years ago. For most effective results, these sounds should not be voiced at all. They should be whispered silently as though you are voicing them but without engaging the vocal chords.

You can hear the sounds in your mind as you chant them. Your mouth should seek to form the sounds, your throat may seek to form the sounds, but no actual vocalized sound should escape except for perhaps some very slight breath sound. But, as you master this technique and learn to release the air slowly enough, not even the sound of breath will be heard. The mastery of breath is the mastery of the mind and the emotions. So, as you practice this technique, work toward releasing your breath slowly and evenly and silently.

The Five Element Breaths are followed by a sixth breath which unifies all six sounds and helps to bind them together. This is also the sound in the Germanic Runic tradition (Isa) for the integration of the complete personality.

The Six Breath Practice
Before beginning the practice, relax the body and mind. Stand comfortably with the arms at the sides and relax the body. Exhale any stale breath from your lungs. Allow the eyes to close, focus attention on the third eye above the nose, inhale deeply through the nose and then whisper the sounds silently out the mouth. Allow the breath to escape slowly. Chant each sound 3, 6 or 9 times before moving on to the next sound.

Here are the six sounds and they should be practiced in this progression:

Shhh (Wood/Aether)
Haaa (Fire)
Huuu (Earth)
Ssss (Metal/Air)
Fuuu (Water)
Eeee (Central Channel)

Do each breath at least three times. But, don't overdo it at first. This is a very powerful method of Energy work. When you are finished, place your hands over your navel and breathe long and deep allowing the energy to accumulate in the navel where it can be processed and stored.

This breath method uses the Gathering Cycle of Elemental progression.

Shhh is the sound for **Aether** and transforms any feelings of resentment stored in the Liver and creates a sense of fairness. **Haaa** is the **Fire** sound and transforms any impatience in Heart Center into Love. **Huuu** is the **Earth** sound and transforms any feelings of stress or confusion in the digestive tract into a sense of comprehension and understanding. **Ssss** is the sound for **Air** and transforms any feelings of sadness in the Lungs into a sense of tranquil intuition. **Fuuu** is the sound of **Water** that transforms any feelings of fear in the kidneys into an attitude of practical resourcefulness. **Eee** is the sound of the Central Channel which unifies the Five Elements in the Body.

(The "F" sound for the Water can be more like a "ph" sound using just the lips pursed together as opposed to using the teeth on the upper lip as is normally done with the "F" letter. But, either way will work just fine.)

Advanced Thunder Wheel Five Element Breaths

After you have practiced the above method a few times, you can use this technique in the Thunder Wheel at the beginning of your rituals in order to empower your sacred space.

Start by facing East and silently chanting "Shhhh." Then, turn to the South and silently chant "Haaa." Then, stay facing South but focus your intention toward centering the Energy beneath your feet in the center of the circle and chant "Huuu." Then, face West and silently chant "Ssss." Then face North and silently chant "Fuuu." Lastly, stay facing North but imagine energy descending down through the top of your head through the center of your body and silently chant "Eeee."

When you are finished, place your hands over your navel center and spend a few moments allowing this energy to accumulate in your Navel center where it can be processed and stored for later use. As you are in this last stage of the practice, you can bring to mind any intentions you wish to manifest or imagine any problems resolving themselves.

The Earth Mother

The first religions found all over the world are rooted in worship of Mother Earth. Anyone wishing to progress as a Thunder Shaman will need to be initiated by Mother Earth Herself. This is what we will accomplish next.

After almost two decades of practice and research, I experienced a very powerful shamanic initiation process connecting me personally to the primordial Earth Mother. In meditative vision, I was given a sacred sound, posture, breath and visualization which connected me to Mother Earth in a most powerful way. When done correctly, this technique will put you in a deep shamanic trance instantly.

The initiation you will receive right now is a self-initiation into the power of the primordial Mother. The tribal shamans of Northern Europe called the Earth Mother "Hulda." The root of her name is "HUUL." We can instantly connect to her immense power through the ancient and sacred sound of HUL .(pronounced 'HUUUUL' with a long U sound similar to the word "Who'll")

The First letter (H): This sound represents the original matrix of primordial creation. It is the static perfection of the blueprint of the universe as embodied in the primordial ice from whence all life originated.

The second letter (U): This sound signifies the raw primordial power of life force descending to Earth in rain. This is the power of the unmanifested universe as it descends into manifested form. It is used for both healing and for protection.

The third letter (L): This sound represents the primordial waters of creation under the earth. This is the water of life that bursts forth in springs. It is the immensity of the ocean. It is the essence of the waters of life. It represents nourishing, cleansing and healing.

Each one of these letters independently is a powerful and healing syllable, but when put together in this order (HUL) they represent an extremely powerful combination of primal energy and immense power. Chanting these sounds in this order represents a cycle of healing, cleansing and rebirth. The H sound initiates an infusion of highly charged, pure, unmanifested Life Force Energy from the heavens. The U sound pulls that pure, heavenly energy descending into manifestation. This highly charged perfect energy descends all the way down through our bodies and into the depths of the Earth. The L sound infuses the waters of Life deep in the center of the Earth with this highly charged Life Force Energy. The waters at the depths of the earth begin to boil and release a powerful steam which rises up through the soil up into the atmosphere and becomes clouds which create rain, hail and snow which once again descend to earth to heal, nurture and cleanse all life in the Cosmos and the process is repeated.

When I chant this sound, I imagine the powers of Mother Earth unleashed onto the planet in a primordial rain that washes away the pollution in the physical realm as well as on the psychic and emotional realms. For me, I can think of no better sacred sound to use as a remedy for the soul-sickness of modern human civilization. HUL is a sound that can heal us from detachment from Mother Earth and from the cancer of unconscious self-hatred. Below is one meditation for using the power of HUL as a means of empowerment and healing. It can also be a powerful form of magic when used as a weapon against unconscious destruction.

Earth Mother (HUUL) Meditation
Sit comfortably in a chair with your feet flat on the ground. Your back should be comfortably straight but not rigid. Look downwards in front of your feet. This will naturally extend the back of the neck. Place your hands at your sides next to your hips with the palms facing down, fingers pointing forward as though you are going to push yourself up from a bench.

Earth Meditation Standing Posture

Imagine that you have tennis balls in your underarms, so that your arms will not be flush against your ribs. Opening the underarms will stimulate energy flow in the arms. Feel the earth beneath your feet and simultaneously put your concentration on the center of your palms and on the soles of your feet. On the inhale, imagine a cool mist entering through the crown of your head and descending to your heart center. Then exhale while slowly and silently chanting the sound *"HUUL."* As you chant the sound, feel the healing mist trickle down through your body and exit through the palms and the heels all the way to the center of the Earth where it forms into a large subterranean lake. As you are completing the exhale and making the *"L"* sound with your tongue touching the roof of your mouth (allow your tongue to touch the actual roof of your mouth, this will stimulate the pineal gland), imagine the subterranean lake bubbling and creating a mist that rises up into the atmosphere and freezes into clouds high above your head. Then inhale and allow the icy snowflakes to descend and melt into a cool, healing mist that once again enters your crown. And the cycle repeats itself. Continue like this for as long as you wish. This is a very healing meditation. You can also imagine the power of HUUL healing and restoring the Earth while simultaneously healing the communal psyche of humanity, bringing society back to Earth consciousness.

Shamanic Journeying To The Nine Worlds

In this next section we will explore shamanic journeying techniques to each of the Nine Worlds. The Nine Worlds exist both in the external Macrocosm of the manifested Cosmos and in the internal Microcosm of the individual. Through Shamanic journeying, we can integrate both the internal and external worlds.

Shamanic Journeying Methods

There are an infinite number of methods to achieve an altered state of consciousness. For simplicity's sake, I will teach you how to use breath to achieve an altered state of consciousness conducive to shamanic journeying.

But before I continue, I want to state that it is not necessary to experience an exaggerated altered state of mind and body to achieve a deeply shamanic state. So, in the beginning, don't worry too much about "feeling" anything. In my experience, some of the most profound shamanic communications have been very subtle in nature. It's also fine if you do have a powerful experience. We are not doing this for an experience, we are doing this to allow ourselves to be transformed. If you do these exercises properly, whether you feel anything or not, I can assure you that you are being transformed on multiple levels. If you are consistent in these practices, you will begin to notice profound changes in your awareness and perception in ways you may not immediately notice. But over time, if you look back, you will see that you have changed and that your life has begun moving in different directions also…

Shamanic Breath Technique
This next technique is a breath technique I developed which is designed to prepare the nervous system and body for achieving a shamanic state of mind. The goal is very simple; allow the breath technique to do the work. Don't try and do anything. Nothing has to happen. Your only goal should be to allow the power of breath to relax and nurture you.

For the purposes of this chapter, you are going to use this technique to create a connection between yourself and whichever direction/world you are working with. For example, if you are seeking to journey to the Northern World of Primordial Waters, you would sit comfortably in a chair or on the ground and face North. It is important that you be comfortable. Sitting comfortably in a chair is the easiest method for most people. However, if you are trained in a certain type of meditation posture such as Yogic full lotus, Taoist or Buddhist meditation, feel free to employ that method also. But, sitting in a comfy chair works just as well…

Facing North in whatever posture you choose, close your eyes and begin breathing long and deep. Allowing the diaphragm (belly) to expand fully with each breath and release fully on each exhale. When your breathing has become relaxed, natural and full, exhale all the "stale" air out of your lungs with a complete exhale and then begin this breath method:

Inhale to a count to five, hold the breath for a count of three, exhale for a count of five and hold the breath out for a count of one. Repeat for at least 3 minutes.

So before we go into shamanic journeying with the directions, let's just get used to this breath technique and use it as a meditation. For this we are just going to sit or lie down anywhere and just practice the following breath technique, **Inhale** "one thousand one, one thousand two, one thousand three, one thousand four, one thousand five." **Hold In** "one thousand one, one thousand two, one thousand three. **Exhale** "one thousand one, one thousand two, one thousand three, one thousand four, one thousand five." **Hold Out** "one thousand one."

Repeat like this for at least three minutes or as long as you like. This is a great meditation in and of itself. You may fall asleep. That's OK too. When you feel comfortable with this breath technique, you can begin the journeys to the directions...

This is a very relaxed form of shamanism. I will give some minimal guidance into what you can choose to imagine to start off your journey, but please don't feel you have to adhere to my suggestions. Allow whatever imagery or experience arise that works for you. The Nine Realms are real but the symbolism of each World may appear differently to different people.

So, you need not impose anything onto your experience and at the same time, you need not limit your experiences either. Don't expect anything and don't judge anything, just observe and see what happens. It's OK if you feel or experience nothing. The meditation is still working and the powers of the directions are communicating with you perhaps on deeper levels beneath your conscious awareness. You can analyze and meditate on the meanings of the visions or lack thereof after the journey. In fact, it is recommended that you do just that.

You may receive information in your journey that makes no sense to you at all. But, after meditating on what you receive, you will very likely find some very profound teaching that can guide your life in ways you never expected. This is the nature of true shamanic journeys. For me, it often takes months or years to interpret what I have received. My entire body of written work is a direct result of a shamanic journey I took years ago that I am still deciphering and interpreting. So, don't minimize any experiences you have. Having said that, you don't need to overemphasize them either. Just observe....

My suggestion is to start with the North, the realm of unmanifested potential and proceed in a clockwise fashion until you have journeyed to each direction. After journeying to each of the eight directions, then take a journey inward which will be the "middle earth" realm within you.

North
The Realm of Primordial Ice and Water.

Begin your shamanic breathing and continue for at least 3 minutes. When you feel yourself enter a shamanic state of mind, you can begin your journey. You can imagine yourself traveling on water. You can also ask for a guide to meet you and take you into the Northern World. The Northern Realm is very powerful and it is suggested that you find a guide who can safely guide you into the realm of unmanifested potential. To summon your guide, simply state either aloud or in your mind that you wish to travel to the Northern World of Mist. Ask that a benevolent guide from the Northern World come to you and guide you. Then wait for any image to come to your mind. You need not impose any experience, but if you begin to find yourself imagining a journey to the Northern World, you may ask your guide any questions. When you have finished your Journey, return to your chair in this reality. Immediately write down anything that was said to you by any beings you encountered or any experiences you had while in this realm. Whether or not it makes any sense to you, there is very likely some important information contained in your dialogue with otherworldly inhabitants.

NorthEast
The Realm of The Highest Heavens

Begin your shamanic breathing and continue for at least 3 minutes. When you feel yourself enter a shamanic state of mind, you can begin your journey. You can imagine yourself ascending a tall mountain. You can also ask for a guide to meet you and take you into the Upper World. To summon your guide, simply state either aloud or in your mind that you wish to travel to the World of the Celestial gods. Ask that a benevolent guide from the Upper World come to you and guide you. Then wait for any image to come to your mind. The realm of the highest heavens can be overwhelming in its brilliance, but the residents there are committed to your highest destiny so you can feel free to interact with them. You need not impose any experience, but if you begin to find yourself imagining a journey to the Upper World, you may ask your guide any questions. When you have finished your Journey, return to your chair in this reality. Immediately write down anything that was said to you by any beings you encountered or any experiences you had while in this realm. Whether or not it makes any sense to you, there is very likely some important information contained in your dialogue with otherworldly inhabitants.

East
The Realm of Thunder And Lightning

Begin your shamanic breathing and continue for at least 3 minutes. When you feel yourself enter a shamanic state of mind, you can begin your journey. You can imagine yourself traveling East toward the rising sun and entering a thick forest. You can also ask for a guide to meet you at the edge of the forest and take you safely through the Realm of the giants and guide you to the ruler of Thunder and Lightning. The giants can be aggressive toward humans, but if you are clear about your intentions, your guide will protect you. Your goal in the Western world should not be to interact with the giants but to reach the Master of Thunder and gain a gift of power. To summon your guide, simply state either aloud or in your mind that you wish to travel to the Realm of Thunder and Lightning. Ask that a benevolent guide from the Eastern World come to you and guide you. Then wait for any image to come to your mind. When you reach the Ruler of Thunder, you may ask for special protection or a gift of Power as this is his job… to protect and empower you… You need not impose any experience, but if you begin to find yourself imagining a journey to the Eastern World, you may ask your guide any questions. When you have finished your Journey, return to your chair in this reality. Immediately write down anything that was said to you by any beings you encountered or any experiences you had while in this realm. Whether or not it makes any sense to you, there is very likely some important information contained in your dialogue with otherworldly inhabitants. If the Master of Thunder gave you an object of power, you may want to look for that same object in the real world and keep it in a safe place or upon your alter or even wear it as a talisman.

SouthEast
The Realm Of Magic And Intention

Begin your shamanic breathing and continue for at least 3 minutes. When you feel yourself enter a shamanic state of mind, you can begin your journey. You can imagine yourself entering a cave cut into the side of a mountain. This is the realm of the masters of the subconscious, the masters of Intention. You can also ask for a guide to meet you and take you into the World of the Dwarves. To summon your guide, simply state either aloud or in your mind that you wish to travel to the Realm of Intention. Ask that a benevolent guide from the SouthEastern World come to you and guide you. Then wait for any image to come to your mind. You need not impose any experience, but if you begin to find yourself imagining a journey to the World of Magic, you may ask your guide any questions. The Subconscious is a tricky realm. The residents there may try to trick you. So, it may be best to allow your guide to act as mediator with the residents of the SouthWest. Follow his/her guidance and only interact with Dwarves that he/she deems as safe. When you have finished your Journey, return to your chair in this reality. Immediately write down anything that was said to you by any beings you encountered or any experiences you had while in this realm. Whether or not it makes any sense to you, there is very likely some important information contained in your dialogue with otherworldly inhabitants.

South

The Realm of Transformation By Fire

Begin your shamanic breathing and continue for at least 3 minutes. When you feel yourself enter a shamanic state of mind, you can begin your journey. You can either imagine yourself in front of a fire or you may actually use a candle or a fireplace. Whether you choose to use real or imaginary fire, stare into the flame. You can also ask for a guide to meet you and take you into the fire. To summon your guide, simply state either aloud or in your mind that you wish to travel to the Realm of Fire and Transformation. Ask that a benevolent guide from the Southern World come to you and guide you. Then wait for any image to come to your mind. This is a good Realm to seek to be released from aspects of your personality that are no longer serving you. You can imagine these things being burned away and released into the atmosphere. It is also a good realm to embrace and empower your forms of expression. If you have been hindering beneficial aspects of your personality, this is a good realm to allow them to come to the surface and be released. Here you can learn to embrace and celebrate your uniqueness and forms of self-expression… You need not impose any experience, but if you begin to find yourself imagining a journey to the World of Fire, you may ask your guide any questions. When you have finished your Journey, return to your chair in this reality. Immediately write down anything that was said to you by any beings you encountered or any experiences you had while in this realm. Whether or not it makes any sense to you, there is very likely some important information contained in your dialogue with otherworldly inhabitants.

SouthWest
Realm Of The UnderWorld

Begin your shamanic breathing and continue for at least
3 minutes. When you feel yourself enter a shamanic
state of mind, you can begin your journey. You can
imagine yourself above a deep well or at the entrance to
an underground cavern. It is recommended that you ask
for a guide to meet you and take you into the
Underworld. The HUUL breath is also a powerful way to
safely enter the Underworld realm. Hulda, the Earth
Mother is a very good guide into this realm. To summon
your guide, simply state either aloud or in your mind that
you wish to travel to the Underworld. Ask that a
benevolent guide from the SouthWest Realm come to
you and guide you. Then wait for any image to come to
your mind. The Underworld can be a challenging place
because of its connection to the deep unconscious.

Residents of this realm may seek to trap you there or follow you out. This is not advised. Use caution when interacting with residents of this Realm. Allow your guide to act on your behalf as a mediator and translator between you and the residents of the Underworld... You need not impose any experience, but if you begin to find yourself imagining a journey to the Underworld, you may ask your guide any questions. When you have finished your Journey, return to your chair in this reality. Immediately write down anything that was said to you by any beings you encountered. Whether or not it makes any sense to you, there is very likely some important information contained in your dialogue with otherworldly inhabitants.

West

Realm Of Fertility And Earth Spirits

Begin your shamanic breathing and continue for at least 3 minutes. When you feel yourself enter a shamanic state of mind, you can begin your journey. You can imagine yourself facing West toward the setting Sun. The Western Realm is often associated with Fertility, Nature and calm bodies of water. So you can imagine a peaceful lake in a beautiful forest... You can also ask for a guide to meet you and take you into the realm of the Fertility spirits. To summon your guide, simply state either aloud or in your mind that you wish to travel to the Realm of the West. Ask that a benevolent guide from the Western World come to you and guide you. Then wait for any image to come to your mind. You need not impose any experience, but if you begin to find yourself imagining a journey to the West, you may ask your guide any questions. The residents of the West are very friendly, feel free to interact with them and ask questions. When you have finished your Journey, return to your chair in this reality. Immediately write down anything that was said to you by any beings you encountered. Whether or not it makes any sense to you, there is very likely some important information contained in your dialogue with otherworldly inhabitants.

NorthWest
Realm of The Ascended Masters

Begin your shamanic breathing and continue for at least 3 minutes. When you feel yourself enter a shamanic state of mind, you can begin your journey. You can imagine yourself facing the Full Moon. The NorthWestern Realm is often associated with Moonlight and Ascended Masters. You can also ask for a guide to meet you and take you into the realm of the Ascended Masters. Or you may wish to simply enter the full Moon. To summon your guide, simply state either aloud or in your mind that you wish to travel to the Realm of the Ascended Masters. Ask that a benevolent guide from the NorthWestern World come to you and guide you. Then wait for any image to come to your mind. You need not impose any experience, but if you begin to find yourself imagining a journey to the NorthWest, you may ask your guide any questions. The NorthWest Realm is probably the safest of all the Nine Realms. The residents of the NorthWest are very friendly and eager to interact with you and help you since that is their main purpose in this reality. So, feel free to interact with them and ask questions. When you have finished your Journey, return to your chair in this reality. Immediately write down anything that was said to you by any beings you encountered. Whether or not it makes any sense to you, there is very likely some important information contained in your dialogue with otherworldly inhabitants. If I had to pick one Realm to travel to, it would absolutely be the NorthWest. The Ascended Masters are the spiritual teachers of Mankind.

Center
Realm Of Middle Earth

Begin your shamanic breathing and continue for at least 3 minutes. When you feel yourself enter a shamanic state of mind, you can begin your journey. You can imagine yourself going inward into the core of your being. For many, this is the heart. It is the Heart Center that houses the "middle self," the Eternal Soul that has come to this realm of Middle Earth in order to have a human experience. You do not need a guide to your own heart for it is YOU who lords over your own Soul. For this, you are free to simply imagine sitting in the center of all the Nine Worlds. Imagine energetic strings from all of the Eight Directions intersecting here in your Heart Center. Imagine yourself being empowered on all levels of your being. You have now connected all Nine of the Worlds on the Sacred Tree of Life. You are known by all of the beings in each realm and each realm can come to your assistance to help you walk your path in this lifetime. As always You need not impose any experience, but if you begin to find yourself imagining a journey into your own sacred heart, you may ask your higher self any questions… When you have finished your Journey, return to your chair in this reality. Immediately write down anything that was said to you by your Higher Self. Whether or not it makes any sense to you, there is very likely some important information contained in your dialogue with otherworldly inhabitants.

Continued Shamanic Journeys

Congratulations! Now that you have traveled to all Nine Worlds of the World Tree, you have connected yourself to all Nine Spiritual Realms and you are now aware of your multi-dimensional essence. You also have a blueprint that you can use to make more shamanic journeys. This is the beginning of a lifetime adventure. You can make regular journeys to the Nine Realms for many different reasons. Once you can become proficient in this, you may find that it is easier and easier to communicate with the Nine Realms. After enough practice, you may be able to connect with the Nine Worlds without any ritual or technique at all.

In my experience, this practice has a cumulative effect. That is why it is OK not to have any experience at first. Over time, you will accumulate enough power that you will notice a change.

This first round of journeys was intended to help you become acquainted with the multiple levels of existence in the manifested Cosmos as well as help you become aware of the multidimensional nature of your internal Universe.

In future journeys, you may want to bring a specific intention, task or question to your journey. The main goal of Shamanic Journeys is not just for personal entertainment. The main goal of these journeys is to effect real, objective change in your life and environment. Shamans for millennia have used this method of spiritual travel to solve all kinds of problems in the "real world."

So, whenever there is a problem in your life, you can journey to other realms of existence and find answers. The advanced level of this practice is to use your connections in the various realms to summon those powers into your life and into manifested existence to help achieve balance and evolution for the world.

Using the power of the Nine Worlds in ritual is an extremely powerful way to effect change and balance in the manifested world. But, before you can summon these powers to effect our lives and environments, we first have to become introduced to these worlds and become familiar with the powers that dwell therein.

The shaman acts as a prism where all the various forces of the Nine Worlds can be channeled. When there is imbalance in the "real world" it mirrors an imbalance with one or more of the Nine Worlds. By regular communication with the Nine Realms, we can regularly bring a dynamic balance to our external world. This balance may represent physical healing, emotional healing and even changes in our world. There is no limit to what can be accomplished. But, in order for us to be effective channels, we must first become clear within ourselves. When we are clear, we can better channel the forces of the Nine Worlds into our reality. So, this is the first task set before us; to use these exercises to achieve a dynamic balance and state of peace within ourselves so that we can be better channels of spiritual balance to those around us.

For those that wish to, you may want to use some kind of sound to enhance your shamanic journeys. Getting a frame drum and drumming before your journeys can help a great deal. Or you can play recordings of shamanic drumming which can be found very easily. Playing flutes before journeying is also helpful. There are many rituals that can be performed before journeys that can be very helpful in attracting the entities in other dimensional realms who can aid in your journeys. Keep your eye on the ThunderShamanism.com homepage for further tools such as guided meditations and drumming recordings which will be provided later.

Personal Mantra

During a ritual meditation years ago, I received a chant that has been very powerful for me. You could call it my personal poem, mantra or even my "song." It connects me directly to my personal Orlog (an ancient word for personal destiny which means "Origin Law"). Whenever I chant this phrase, I can feel that I am activating the power of my personal destiny located in my DNA.

If you wish, you may use my song until you are given your own. It is customary in some traditions to be given a mantra by one's teacher. It allows the student to tap into the energy and blessings of the lineage. If you find this book helpful, you are welcome to self-initiate into this lineage of Thunder Shamanism that I am teaching. One powerful step to self-initiation is to chant the mantra of your teacher. Here is my song. It is very short, nothing fancy, but it contains the essence of my path and the purpose of my teachings. I freely give it to you to use as your own or as a temporary song until you receive yours in vision or dream…

Light descends into me from the Heavens above and shines out as through a diamond in all directions; healing, enlightening and transforming the world.

As you may notice, this chant is rather short and simple. To be honest, when I received it, I was a little disappointed at first. I was expecting something longer and more dramatic. But, when I meditated on the words, I realized it encapsulated very concisely what my mission was in this life. Whenever I need empowerment or to be refocused on my path, I will chant this little phrase and envision what the words describe happening to me. I envision a bright white light descending into my crown chakra (the top of the head), filling my entire being and then shining out of me like light through a prism in every direction filling the entire Universe with the power of spiritual evolution. This little chant acts as my personal road map. It drives away confusion and brings me joy.

If you feel inclined, you may adopt this chant as your own. But, it can also be used to guide you to your own song and your own destiny. In any case, it can light your way on to this path I call "Thunder Shamanism." It will connect you to my guides who can further guide you onto your own path.

Finding Your Own Song

Many shamanic traditions encourage people to seek for a "song" that is given to them in journeys, dreams or meditation. In my experience, the NorthWest realm of the Ascended Masters is a very good direction to seek a personal song.

Here is one suggestion on how you can find your song: Get prepared for a journey to the NorthWest. It is often helpful to bring a gift for your journey. You are seeking a gift from the Ascended Ones, so it is only fitting that you bring a gift to them also…

For this Journey, I am going to suggest that you offer a small quartz crystal as a gift to the Ascended Masters. It doesn't matter where you get the crystal. You can search for one in Nature, find one online or look for one in a local store. If you find a crystal that speaks to you and "wants" you to take it, this is your gift to the Shining Ones.

Journey to Request Your Song
Spend some time meditating about receiving your own song. Contemplate what you want your song to accomplish for you. When you feel clear about what you want to accomplish with your song, you are ready to take a journey to the NorthWest realm.

Set up your chair or meditation mat in your sacred space facing the NorthWest. Place your quartz crystal that you are giving to the Ascended Masters in front of you. Play your drum, or your flute if you choose to do so. If you like to set an atmosphere, light your candles, incense or whatever you like to do to set the mood in your sacred space.

Now you can take your journey to seek your personal song... If you choose to, you can take this journey during a full moon. In my experience, the day before a full moon is the most powerful time to gain the energy of the moon. At the actual day of the full moon, the moon has already peaked and is beginning to wane. The day before full is when the moon is most potent. However, you can choose to take this journey whenever you like. I received my song during an eclipse. So, there is no set rule here...

Begin your shamanic breathing and continue for at least 3 minutes. When you feel yourself enter a shamanic state of mind, you can begin your journey. You can imagine yourself facing the Full Moon. Call for your guide to appear. When he/she does appear, state that you are seeking to receive your own song or chant to help you better walk your path of destiny. Let your guide take you on your journey. Perhaps your guide will take you to someone else to ask for your song or maybe your guide will give it to you. When you have reached the person who is to give you your song, offer them the crystal you have brought as a gift. Then ask for your song. It may be very simple, maybe not... It may be one word or a whole paragraph... If you are having trouble hearing a song, just ask for one word. More may come later... You may or may not understand what your word or phrase means. As in all journeys, do not judge what does or does not happen. Just observe. When your journey is ending, thank your guides and return to your chair in this dimension. Write down whatever you have observed.

Most likely, even though you gave your crystal as a gift to your song guide, there will still be a physical crystal in this dimension still sitting in front of you where you left it. This is now your Power Crystal. It contains the essence of your Power Chant. It has been blessed by your personal guides. Perhaps your guide has taken up residence in that crystal. It will empower your rituals, meditations and journeys. You can wear it as a necklace, place it on your altar, put it in a medicine pouch. You can hold it during your meditations. You can use it at any time to summon your guide to come and protect you.

Quartz is a very powerful channel to expand intention. This is why people use quartz wands in ceremonies.,, The uses for this Power Crystal are infinite. Let your guide and intuition show you all the ways your Power Crystal wants to be used…

Bodily Location of the Nine Worlds

The External Nine Worlds have corresponding locations on the human body. Having a direct connection to the Nine Worlds also keeps these meridian points on the human body activated and healthy.

North: Perineum (Base of Torso)
NorthEast: Crown Chakra (Top of head)
East: Sexual Center (genitals)
SouthEast: Third Eye
South: Navel
SouthWest: Lips/Roof of Mouth
West: Solar Plexus (Where Rib Cage Meets Diaphragm)
NorthWest: Throat
Center: Heart Chakra

By touching each of these locations in this order while facing each corresponding direction in a clockwise fashion, a "Sine Wave" is created which opens a dynamic interconnection between the practitioner's Life Force Energy points (chakras) with the Nine Worlds.

I teach a very detailed version of this practice to open the Nine Worlds and manifest desires. The ancient Anglo-Saxons used a spell to open the Nine Worlds called the "Spell of the Nine Knots." My version of that ancient technique can be found on the instructional DVD entitled "Anglo-Saxon Shamanism - Spell of the Nine

Knots" which can be found in this link https://www.createspace.com/382579 in the resources section at the end of this book on the homepage of the thunderwizard.com website or by searching for it on Amazon.

Apprenticeship

This book is meant as an introduction, an initiation into the path of Thunder Shamanism. While the techniques in this book can be used for a lifetime, there are many other very specific shamanic techniques to achieve Power. Many of these, I have shared in my previous books and DVDs, but the most powerful techniques can only be taught through personal instruction. You are free to use all of the resources I have provided and will continue to provide on a public level to create your own Path of Power. These techniques are provided to anyone who has an interest. It is my hope that these techniques will inspire others to seek out the ways of the Ancient Ones. It is my hope that these works will give anyone who wishes the power to create their own path of Power.

Sometimes, however, it is good to have a mentor. It is very difficult to put all of my knowledge into book and DVDs. Much of my knowledge can only be revealed through personal instruction. If you feel a calling to work with me on a personal basis, you are invited to investigate becoming an apprentice. Information on personal apprenticeship into the Path of Thunder Shamanism is located on the ThunderShamanism.com website.

Conclusion

There is really no easy way to end this book. This is only the beginning of a long adventure. The teachings, I'm finding, are infinite. It is my hope that if this is the first of my books you have read, you will be inspired to continue on this path of shamanic awareness in whatever ways you are guided to do so. If you have read other of my books, perhaps this book has filled in some more information.

I have listed most of my books and DVDs available to this date in the resources section right after this chapter which can also help you on this journey to shamanic empowerment. If you enjoyed this book, you are encouraged to investigate those other resources to help you create your own Path of Power. It is my personal belief that re-connecting with our ancestral shamanic traditions is essential if we humans are to survive this coming energetic shift that we have already entered.

A New Energetic Shift
According to Vedic belief, our galaxy revolves around a cosmic center where pure Divinity is located. Our galaxy orbits this Divine center in an elliptical fashion. When we are closest to this Divine center, the human population is most closely aligned to pure Divine wisdom and we act accordingly. This is known as the Golden Age where humans are living gods. But, as our galaxy moves away from the Divine Center, we drift further and further from our Divine Essence.

Each 25,000 years we enter into a new "age" of human evolution or de-evolution (depending on whether the galaxy is moving toward or away from the Divine Center). As the galaxy moves farthest from the Divine Center, we enter into what is known as "Kali Yuga" or "Dark Age." My ethnic ancestors described this age as "Ragnarock" where the agents of chaos and destruction ruled. According to Vedic understanding, during Kali Yuga, approximately 75% of human beings are operating from their basest animal urges.

Kali Yuga is known for violence, betrayal and spiritual emptiness. Many believe we are in this dark age. But, thankfully, our Galaxy has begun the return trip toward the Divine Center. We actually began shifting out of Kali Yuga during the Renaissance. It is no coincidence that the Renaissance inspired many humans to begin rediscovering ancient polytheist mythology. But, at first it was only on an intellectual level. Now that we are approaching the Aquarian Age, more and more people are beginning to see that the Old Mythology is also a valuable spiritual resource that can be experienced on a spiritual and even a bodily level. As we get closer to pure Divinity, the gods and spirits of the Ancestors are able to reach and communicate directly with us again. As we enter into the next phase of spiritual evolution, we will enter an age where approximately 50% of humans will be operating from their Divine Essence. Perhaps you have felt a change. Yes, there are many who strongly resist spiritual evolution, but if we examine this trend objectively, we can see that the followers of the past mindset of ignorance and fear are becoming less and less every year.

And people are beginning to wake up!

Some years ago, I was contacted by the gods and Ancestors of my pre-Christian heritage. And I was launched into an intense journey of study and personal development that has altered me beyond my wildest dreams. And I have since found out that I am not alone. I have been contacted by more than a few people who have shared with me that the Ancestors have contacted them in visions and dreams and encouraged them to reconnect with the Ancient Ways.

This is just the beginning. I invite you to join me on this journey to awaken the ancient shamanic understanding of our Ancestors who lived in harmony with their Natural environment. This path of Shamanic Empowerment which I call "Thunder Shamanism" is one way we can accomplish that.

I wish you Power and Joy as you embrace this path. I believe we will meet each other along the way.

May the blessings of the Ancient Ones guide you…

Resources

Here is a list of many of my books and DVDs to date. There will be more coming…

DVDs

Qigong (Energy Work):

Celestial Qigong DVDs 1 and 2
www.SpiritTao.com (click on "Spirit Tao DVD" page)
Celestial Qigong is one of my older DVD series and is perhaps the most potent energy work I have ever taught. It is a distillation of

some of the most powerful qigong (Energy Work) and nei gong (Internal Work) I have ever experienced. Many people have contacted me who have trained in Taoist Energy Work and Martial for many years and expressed that this DVD is as powerful or more so than any other energy work they have experienced. More than one person has shared their experience of meeting Ascended Masters as a result using these techniques. Please be careful with these techniques as they are extremely potent.

Thunder Qigong DVD
http://www.qigong.thundershamanism.com
This is a great DVD combining old school martial qigong, mantra and meditation. This practice will fill the body with powerful Life Force Energy and open the meridians. The mantras and meditations are extremely healing and powerful which can connect you with the source of "Thunder Magic", a great DVD for the Warrior Shaman.

Medicine Wheel Qigong DVDs 1, 2 and 3
http://www.medicinewheel.thundershamanism.com
This three part qigong series is very pertinent to the work in this book. In this series, I teach powerful standing postures for each of the Nine Worlds. Combining this practice with the principles and techniques in this book will give you even more powerful ways to enhance your journeys into the Nine Worlds. Level 1 teaches the basic postures for each direction, Level 2 teaches how to integrate all 10 postures into a fluid practice and Level 3 teaches some very important info on how to balance the "spiritual" directions to achieve psychological and emotional balance which can later be used in shamanic ritual to achieve balance in the real world.

Shamanism and Energy Work

Thunder Shamanism DVD
https://www.createspace.com/375307
This DVD has more information about creating a stone Medicine Wheel altar or "Thunder Wheel" for rituals. This DVD expands on a lot of the information in this book. This DVD also includes magical hand seals or mudras which can energetically be used to empower and channel each of Five Elements and the eight directions.

Anglo-Saxon Shamanism - Spell of the Nine Knots DVD

This DVD reviews info from the Thunder Shamanism DVD and then teaches a very powerful shamanic method of opening the gates to the Nine Worlds by connecting various points on the body with each of the Eight Directions and the Nine Worlds of the Tree of Life. Then, I teach a modern interpretation of an Ancient Anglo-Saxon magical chant known as " The Spell of the Nine Knots." This ancient spell was used by pre-Christian Anglo Saxon witches to manifest desires and it is said these witches had the power to control the weather using this spell. This is one of my favorite shamanic techniques to open the powers of the Nine Worlds to manifest desires. The techniques in the DVD are extremely powerful. Continued practice in this technique can eventually make one into a very powerful warrior shaman who can effect change into the real world.

Sanskrit Mantra and Meditation

Chakras - Wheels of Transformation - Part 1 DVD

Chakras - Wheels of Transformation - Part 2 DVD

This is one of my older DVD series I made a few years ago that teaches some great information on the Chakras. It also teaches a powerful yogic breath meditation to open the "nadis" or energy meridians and clean out old stuck energy. This is a staple breath meditation or "pranayama" (Breath/Energy Work) taught to yogis for centuries. In this series, I also teach a powerful mantra for the feminine Power of the Sun called the Gayatri Mantra. This is perhaps the most chanted mantra in the history of the world. It is a very ancient mantra for spiritual evolution used by both hindus and buddhists all over the world. This is the lesser known "long" version of the mantra which opens all of the seven main chakras in the body. This DVD is a must for any serious shaman or yogi.

Ganesha Mantras DVD

The deity known as Lord Ganesha in Vedic/Hindu ritual is always worshipped before any new action or project. Vedic mythology states that even Shiva, the Lord of the gods must worship his son Ganesha before any action. Shiva states that even he cannot accomplish anything without Ganesha's approval. The root of the name Ganesha (Gam) comes from the same root for the English word "go." Ganesha is the principle that makes things "go", that sets them in motion. This DVD teaches various mantras for the power of manifestation otherwise known as "Ganesha."

Mythology

The Voluspa DVD Part 1
https://www.createspace.com/386794

The Voluspa DVD Part 2
https://www.createspace.com/386857

The Voluspa DVD Part 3
https://www.createspace.com/386862

The Voluspa (The Prophecy of the Seeress) is one of the most important religious texts of Pre-Christian Norse polytheism. Originally transcribed during the introduction of Christianity to Scandinavia, this sacred poem preserves the original spiritual beliefs of the indigenous polytheist Germanic tribes of northwestern Europe. In this 3-part video teaching series, I examine the underlying spiritual and mystical symbolism contained within the Voluspa. The Voluspa is considered to be a creation myth,and indeed it is, but from a mystical perspective, this is a veiled mystery teaching about the evolution of the Human race from mere animal into divine deity. In this series, you will learn the hidden shamanic understanding of the Aesir (celestial deities), the Vanir (deities of procreation), Dwarves (powers of self-awareness), Elves (ascended masters), Giants (powers of the laws of physics), Thurses (forces of self-sabotage) and the fire demon Surt (the force of entropy). Mr. Denney will also reveal a shocking origin for the god Odin (shamanic awareness) that I guarantee you, will shock you to your core. Most importantly, the Voluspa foretells the inevitable evolution of Human beings from knuckle dragging apes into the highest of celestial deities. Whatever you may think you know about pre-Christian European religion, prepare to have your mind expanded. Whatever your religious background, you deserve to know what our ancestors really believed about the human race and

why this secret teaching was suppressed by the Christian church.
The gods are you!

Books

The Thunder Wizard Path
https://www.createspace.com/3534639

This is one of my first books where I share my shamanic experiences
meeting my ancestral teachers who revealed to me some lost
knowledge concerning the shamanic beliefs of my ethnic European
ancestors. Even though I had been studying, teaching and practicing
shamanic practices from Asia, India and Africa, my final initiation into
shamanic power came from the spirits of my European ancestors.
This book launched me into an amazing journey into very ancient
shamanic knowledge spanning to the dawn of modern human
beings.

Wealth Shaman
https://www.createspace.com/3601650
(I believe this was my first book I self published. A great book that
explains the shamanic process…)
Are you a spiritually inclined person who is conflicted when it comes
to money?
Have you tried to make a living through Spirit Friendly ways, but
have gotten nowhere because modern society doesn't seem to
understand what you offer to the world?
There is a way to celebrate your spiritual uniqueness and make a
good living. I'm NOT talking about a re-hashed version of "The
Secret" or some other New Age gimmick like subliminal CD's, self
hypnosis, life coaching or positive affirmations. I'm talking about
ancient shamanic principles of living that can create abundant
prosperity and allow you to be spiritually fulfilled expressing your true
spiritual gifts.

Awakening Sleipnir
https://www.createspace.com/3634086
It is imperative that we examine our modern assumptions about how
our tribal, pre-Christian European ancestors perceived and interfaced

with the Cosmos. "Awakening Sleipnir" explores how we modern "civilized" Westerners can awaken this ancient understanding within ourselves...

"I realized that I was furious at my ancestors who abandoned the Old Ways. I was furious that they had discarded MY ancestral animist traditions. What right did they have erasing our indigenous shamanic practices? Those were MY practices too and I wanted the right to make my own choice regarding whether or not I wanted to follow them. I was furious and embarrassed that as a result of their choice hundreds of years ago, I was now forced to go to other cultural traditions and beg to be taught authentic shamanic practices. .... But, little did I know that my ancestors would reach out through time and thrust me into a new spiritual practice, an ANCIENT practice stretching back to the dawn of tribal European society..."

Mounting Sleipnir
https://www.createspace.com/4059668
"The Germanic names for Indo-European deities seem to reflect an older, more primal version of Indo-European polytheist animism which perhaps reflects the older more "shamanic" version of the original Indo-European religion..."

In this book, I examine the underlying polytheist root religion of the Germanic tribes by uncovering and comparing the linguistic connections of the names of deities in both the Vedic and Germanic religions.

In this book you will learn the linguistic connections to the deities: Thor/Indra, Buri/Brahma, Freyja/Prajaapati, Ing/Agni, Ymir/Yama, Tyr/Dyeus Pita and more... This book also examines the indigenous Germanic deities: Odin,Villi, Ve, Loki and Surt, You will also learn the pre-Christian understanding of Dwarves, Elves, Wights (Nature Spirits), Norns, Thurses, Giants, Valkyries and the mythical horse, Sleipnir.

Rune Shamanism
https://www.createspace.com/4059691
Runes have been used for divination and writing in Europe for thousands of years. But where did they come from? Modern

academia tells us that the Runic alphabet was adopted 2200 years ago. But could they be older than that?... Perhaps much, MUCH older?

In this book, author Michael William Denney closely examines the historical and linguistic mysteries of the Runic alphabet known as the "Elder Futhark." But, this isn't just another re-hashing of the same old academic questions about Rune stave meanings.

Mr. Denney reveals a powerful, ancient method of Rune Shamanism, a FORGOTTEN method of Rune galdor that may have been the original method of Rune magic taught in secret from father to son during the ice ages when the early Germanic tribes were differentiating themselves from their other Indo-European cousins.

"Rune Shamanism" reveals a powerful method of spiritual transformation available to all modern seekers of ancient shamanic wisdom.

Rune Divination
https://www.createspace.com/4341828
Runes are more than the pre-Christian alphabet of Northern Europe. They are the sacred sound syllables that connect us to the Celestial Ancestors - the gods. Through the Runes, we can tap into powerful divine forces that can guide us through our journey in life. For hundreds, perhaps thousands of years, the pre-Christian, pre-Roman, Teutonic tribes of Europe used the Runes to receive guidance from the gods and foretell future events.

In "Rune Divination" author Michael William Denney re-examines the history of the Runic alphabet and asks, "Are the Runes older than we think?" Mr. Denney exposes some outdated theories on the origins of the Runes. He also exposes some of the inaccuracies of modern Rune divination interpretations by comparing them with the actual meanings of the language of the Runes themselves.

The Runic alphabet is more than just a collection of archaic symbols. They are the ancient building blocks of the Germanic languages and windows into the origins of pre-Christian European, Religion, Magic and Shamanism...

Advanced Rune Shamanism
https://www.createspace.com/4286863
Advanced Rune Shamanism is the third in a series of Rune Shamanism books. This latest in the series is a synergistic method of Rune work which combines external Rune divination with internal Rune shamanism. This book also reveals a previously unknown method of Rune casting combining the shamanic pre-Christian European eight direction 'medicine' or sun-wheel, the three levels of existence (Odin, Villi and Ve) and connects them to the nine Worlds of the pre-Christian, tribal European Tree of Life.

The second half of the book is dedicated to a simple, yet profound, intuitive technique of shamanic divination and healing with the Runes that employs a 'counterbalancing' method of divination that can reverse the energy blockages in ones destiny.

Odin says, "Jesus was a coward!"
https://www.createspace.com/4924347
During the middle ages, we Westerners abandoned our polytheist, animist heritage for the dualist, separation contained within monotheist Christianity. In "Odin Says," Michael William Denney shares his personal experiences communicating with a being claiming to be the god Odin. The author also explores and discusses the historical authenticity of the Jesus myth as well as the historical origins of modern monotheism and the massive shift in consciousness of the European psyche. "Odin Says," examines the toxic effects of monotheism on Western culture and the modern world.

Shamanism for "White People"
https://www.createspace.com/4040938
Shamanism is a transcendent practice of dynamic spiritual balance. Shamanism has become increasingly popular in recent decades. But there is a great deal of controversy over the increasing trend of people of European descent practicing shamanism. Many Native spiritual practitioners have accused "white" people of stealing their cultural and spiritual practices. New age charlatans and "plastic shamans" have muddied the waters making it difficult to know what is an authentic shamanic practice for the sincere "white seeker." In "Shamanism for 'White' People," author Michael William Denney explores the current controversies regarding neo-shamanism. In this

book, you will learn about the ancient and profound animist (shamanic) practices of pre-Christian European tribes. Mr. Denney exposes the myths on both sides of this controversy. If you are a "white" person, animism (shamanism) is your spiritual birthright.

Websites

www.ThunderShamanism.com
www.ThunderWizard.com
www.SpiritTao.com
www.Sun-Wheel-Magick.com
www.TheHealingDrum.com

Audio CDs
Healing Drums of Power
http://www.cdbaby.com/cd/thehealingdrum
Healing Mantras
http://www.cdbaby.com/cd/thehealingdrum2
Ancient Earth Mantra (HUUL Breath)
http://www.cdbaby.com/cd/thehealingdrum3

YouTube Channel
https://www.youtube.com/user/
ThunderWizarddotcom

Rune Readings by Phone
http://www.keen.com/psychic-readings/tarot-
readers/askmiked/11893763